T0086848

AMY BEACH
arr. Robert Gower

SCOTTISH LEGEND

MUSIC DEPARTMENT

OXFORD
UNIVERSITY PRESS

Scottish Legend

from *Two Piano Pieces*, Op. 54

AMY BEACH
(1867–1944)
arr. Robert Gower

© Oxford University Press 2019

Printed in Great Britain

OXFORD UNIVERSITY PRESS, MUSIC DEPARTMENT, GREAT CLARENDON STREET, OXFORD OX2 6DP
The Moral Rights of the Composer have been asserted. Photocopying this copyright material is ILLEGAL.

The Oxford Organ Library is an invaluable resource of standalone pieces for today's organist, whether for concerts or church services. It features newly commissioned music, selected pieces from existing OUP anthologies, and canonical works brought back into print by popular demand. The series provides diverse and eminently useful repertoire from composers associated with Oxford and its long tradition of publishing for the organ.

TITLES IN THE OXFORD ORGAN LIBRARY

OXFORD
UNIVERSITY PRESS

www.oup.com

ISBN 978-0-19-353305-9

9 780193 533059

Dance
Caprice

by Christopher Bunting

for Cello and Piano

Oxford University Press